D0558713

SEEING *through* VEILS

SEEING *through* VEILS

A Handbook for Peace and Balance

LORI WHEELER

ARCHWAY
PUBLISHING

Archway Publishing books may be ordered
through booksellers or by contacting:

Archway Publishing
1663 Liberty Drive
Bloomington, IN 47403
www.archwaypublishing.com
1 (888) 242-5904

ISBN: 978-1-4808-4501-5 (sc)
ISBN: 978-1-4808-4502-2 (e)

Library of Congress Control Number: 2017903871

Print information available on the last page.

Archway Publishing rev. date: 3/14/2017

Contents

Dedication

To Paul, Jean (Bugsy), and Sienna.

Thank you for your love and support. Thank you for allowing me the time needed to help the people who need it most.

Many thanks and lots of love ...

To my best friend of forty years, Kimberly Young, for being there every step of the way. You have always been my rock and have given me the love and support I needed to get through this roller coaster journey we call life.

To my dear friends Ellen Goldberg, Kay DeLonge, Jen George, Jenny Ross, Susan Klepper, and Debra Brown for allowing me to continue my work in helping others and accepting me for person I am. This journey would have not been nearly as successful without you guys.

Sincere thanks to every person who has touched my soul and allowed me to help them. I could not do the things I do without you.

Foreword

BY ELLEN CRAWFORD

Did you ever get a feeling that something had a different meaning? That a bird landing closer than normal to you and staying put for longer than normal, was a sign of something else?

When you saw a name or favorite number of a loved one, was he or she saying hello?

Have you gotten a feeling that you should check your purse before you leave to make sure your keys were in the same pocket you always keep them in because you had a fleeting feeling they were not in that pocket? But you ignored the feeling, only to discover when you got to your car that in fact your keys were not in your purse. Then you thought to yourself, *Why didn't I trust my instincts?*

Several years ago, not long after my father died, my sister went to a group reading. The event had been scheduled months prior to my father's passing. She really wanted to back out, but her friends urged her to, mostly because they thought it would be a good distraction from the painful loss of our father.

You know the kind of event, where a medium selects a handful of eager attendees who are hoping for an impactful message from a lost loved one.

My father's passing hit us all very hard. We are a close bunch. So when the medium was reading another attendee and said, "Excuse me, but there's a spirit here who wants to introduce himself and won't take no for an answer," my sister knew who that was.

One of my father's favorite things to do was to introduce himself, no matter how many times he'd met someone. Even in my senior year of college, with roommates he had known for years, he would call and say, "Hi, this is Ron Crawford. Is Ellen there?"

My sister experienced my father, and some of his strongest mannerisms that drove us crazy, which we now all long for, came through. He had a single and important message to deliver: my mother was strong, would get through this, and would be okay. Again, this is totally what my father would do and how he would do it; there was no denying it.

My sister came home that night, overwhelmed with emotion, with sadness and relief, and told my mother. They cried together and realized that the message from my father was real.

Was it real? Was that my pop? Was the medium a hoax? How could she know these things? Doubters never believe what's in front of them or around them or what they're told. Most people follow the guiding principle that seeing is believing.

To me, that expression minimizes our sense of feeling, our heart, our instincts, and what is at the core of our beings. How can we discount our feelings so easily? Believing requires an opening, a cracked door, a sliver of hope, or even the slightest possibility that something could be real.

All of the things the medium said to my sister (her friend took copious notes) left no doubt that my pop wanted to make one thing clear—that my mom would be okay. He delivered his message and was gone. My sister wanted more, but I've learned that's not how it works. We get what we need, and that's all.

When I met Lori, I was at a similar event. One of my friends and his wife were hosting a reading party. My friend's father had recently passed, and he had a session with Lori. The next day, he reached out to me, telling me what an incredible, special, and healing session he had experienced. He encouraged me to have a session with Lori, so when this group reading opportunity arose, I just had to go.

I had always avoided going to psychics in the past as I didn't want to know when I was going to die or when bad things that were going to happen to me. That's what I thought I would hear. My outlook had always been that if it's my time to go, it's my time to go. I don't want to know about it. In actuality, I had no idea what a medium did or what purpose they served.

About twenty-five people attended the group reading, none of whom I knew besides my friend and his wife. Lori started to read each person, some with good news (the ring is behind your jewelry box); some with memories (your grandmother used to whistle while she cooked and always wore the same apron, the one you have now); and some with advice (your decision to tear down the gazebo is correct as it carries negative energy). Each and every time, people were amazed with Lori's words and how they rang true.

Before I arrived at the event, I was extremely excited and anxious to hear what she'd say to me. But as time moved on, fear and apprehension overtook me. By the time she looked my way, I was very uncomfortable and felt strongly that whatever she was going to tell me was not good. And I was right.

She asked me if I had a period of my life I did not remember, and I said yes. She went on to uncover a time very early in my life that I had suppressed, a few years of my life with absolutely no memory at all. I knew I didn't remember; I just never understood why. I had buried all the moments from that time and locked my feelings and my experience in a room I had not even realized was in my house. Compartmentalizing had allowed me to survive all these years. I had suspected something bad happened to me but had never been able to confirm it—nor was I anxious to. As I had no validation, I could keep it locked in that room forever.

Lori only spoke with me for a few minutes. After she was done, I realized I was curled up with my knees under my chin and was crying. It was a painful yet important moment I will not soon forget.

She had spoken out loud what I had been afraid to acknowledge since I was a child. And the events have shaped the person I have become—in both positive and negative ways. What was supposed to be a light and fun event turned into one of the most intense, significant moments of my life.

After the event, I approached Lori and asked if I could see her again as I needed more answers, and I had many more questions. She readily agreed that would be a good step. I scheduled a follow-up session to discover more about the event, expecting the session to be all about my childhood.

What happened moving forward was completely unexpected. In my subsequent visits to Lori, I learned about myself, about the me I am today and how I deal with and approach my life. I learned about the obstacles in my way, many self-imposed. Taking her words seriously, I worked on myself daily. Lori was careful to give me manageable homework and exercises; she didn't give me big tasks. Most of her guidance was about staying present and being aware. I applied her suggestions and advice as I did not want to waste this valuable gift I have been given.

It is quite simple. Lori changed my life. She saved me from darkness. That may sound extreme; I assure you, it is not. I was a mostly happy person. While my external self presented as happy, I was struggling with some major areas. I didn't realize just how much until I started to be more present and open with myself. Lori's advice and direction has been dead-on accurate every time, and I trust her advice with major events in my life. I had no awareness of the darkness I carried with me or how to distance myself from it. She's given me the courage and the tools to be more present, braver, happier, and healthier and to live in a positive place—to live in the moment with light, love, and forgiveness.

There are times when I want for her to tell me what to do. That's my impatience talking, and I know that's not how this works. I get what I need, when I need it; that is all. Now I trust my instincts more. I know the signs that my father is saying hello. Or if my gut tells me to do something, check something, I do and am appreciative of my recognition, as it serves me well in my life.

Lori is not just a medium; she is my spiritual advisor, opening me and many others to the light. There is no way I will ever truly understand the special gifts of Lori or any other medium, and there is also no doubt in my mind that they enrich our world by connecting us to the people, spirits, and energy we need and simply cannot find on our own.

As you read this book, keep an open mind. Allow yourself to be present and to believe. After all, there is a reason you are holding this book in your hands. Believe in empowering yourself in love and light, and it will come your way.

Chapter 1

DOUBLE LINES

I was five when I saw my first apparition. I was in my room and witnessed a dark shadow. Despite the circumstances, it was not scary. This dark shadow turned out to be my guide. By the time I was eight, I was able to fully see my guide, and that continues to this day.

I will include more about my guide throughout the book and will give you tips and suggestions on finding you own guides. For now, I will tell you that my guide goes by the name Chief, and he is an Iroquois Indian from the fifteenth century.

Each guide presents abilities in different ways. My guide presents what I call "double lines" over everyone's head. He calls them blueprints, but they look more like little history lines from an old history book to me, so I am calling them lines.

I label the bottom line the "concrete line" as it starts at about the age of two and continues to the present.

Seeing this line is of great assistance to understand a person's background and to assist when someone comes to me regarding a past traumatic situation (e.g., molestation, illness, accident) or needs more information on an incident that he or she simply can't remember.

I call the top line the "sand line." It picks up from the present day of the visit for a span of about twelve months. This is where people contact me before a relationship, move, job, kids, or any life event that is important and impactful. If you have ever played in the sand, you realize that it isn't concrete and can change at the drop of a hat.

Often I am asked how I can see these lines, speak with Chief, and have this ability. Quite simply, I do not know. I am not the powerful Oz, nor do I understand why I see the lines, but they are there. They have enriched my life by allowing me to aid people in healing from loss or past traumas or in making decisions on current or future situations.

I will discuss people wanting to hear what they want to hear later. It's the same when people ask me about a situation and I give them an answer they may not want to hear. If you come to me and I read in your line that your husband is an abuser and you're in danger, I will tell you! I get to help a lot of abused men and women, and it is my experience that an abuse victim has limited self-esteem, if any, and feels as though he or she can't make it without that person. Telling victims to leave may ring true in their brains, but their hearts make them want to stay. I have had people contact me after the next abuse and say they are ready to leave but don't know how. I get to work with psychotherapists and psychiatrists to help these people have a safe and healthy way out and to learn self-worth once again.

Chapter 2

WHAT DOES "SEEING THROUGH VEILS" MEAN?

The most common topic people talk to me about is my ability to see the people who have crossed over. I have no idea how or why I was chosen to have this ability, but after many years, I have been able to help many people deal with and get through suicides, murders, illnesses, and grief. I am acutely aware that my abilities come with a great deal of responsibility, and I don't take it lightly or for granted.

Unfortunately, as with most blessings, there is another side. I have an enormous amount of anxiety and have found through my travels for networking that many other mediums also have some form of anxiety. *What kind of anxiety? Why? How is it related to being a medium?* Every day is a new day to learn and experience the amazing gift that was given to me.

This book is meant to help you understand what

happens and where your people go when they cross, along with the signs of visits. Many people get stuck or lost when their people cross. The ability to communicate with loved ones who have crossed has given me a great insight that there are other planes, dimensions, or as they call them, veils of life. I will guide you through each veil and what it means.

The pain doesn't end with the comfort of knowing what happens when your people cross though. Many times we find ourselves stuck, bored, sad, and hopeless.

I hope this book helps you continue the grief journey and find peace within your time here.

Every one of us has dealt with some level of grief with losing people. In experiencing grief, we know the effect is both emotional and physical. We often get lost in our own feelings and look for outside acceptance that our feelings are valid. When you lose who you are, you often grieve or yearn for the peace or contentment that comes with that. Consider for one moment whether you know who you really are. I am not asking what you enjoy or if you are stable in life, but who are you? Are you a person who constantly tries to please people or avoid conflict? Do you say that you are the kind, caring person that your (insert relationship) taught you to be? Compassion and empathy are amazing traits that in this world many people lack. While you may donate or volunteer for charities and are left to keep the extended family together, that doesn't tell me who you are. Those are traits—and amazing ones at that—but they don't make you who you are.

Don't think about this next question, but answer as fast as you can: What do you like to do? Okay, simple question, right? Not for everyone. Often in life, if we are emotionally abused or abandoned psychically or mentally, then this is not an easy question, and we feel as though our feelings don't really matter as long as (insert name) is happy or non-confrontational.

So yes, grief is not only from losing a person but also often from losing ourselves when someone we love or care for crosses over. In life, we find people who care for us and love us who give us security. When those people cross, we are left here to figure out how we can move forward without that immediate security blanket. I promise that you can, but only if you give yourself the permission.

Chapter 3

THE FIVE VEILS

If you talk to anyone who does energy work or has an ability to see others, we all relay the same thing but often in different ways. I say that because sometimes people *want* to hear something or from someone, and if it doesn't happen, they keep searching to find it. Most people will never find the answer they *want* to hear, but they will find the answer they are supposed to hear.

There are five veils in the universe. We live in veil one. Your people who cross go to veil two. Spirit guides are in veil three, guardian angels are in veil four, and the higher power is in veil five. It is important to understand that your guardian angel isn't Grandma, and your guide isn't your guardian angel. It can be a bit confusing at first, but don't worry. I'll walk you through each of these veils. It has taken me many years to understand that it isn't just heaven" and "hell. You will notice throughout the book I will rarely use the word *die* or *died.* This is due to the fact that when I chat with your people, they always use the words *cross over* or *transition.* Wait? What? What do you mean when you talk to them?

Veil one is where we all live now. This is where we experience pain, sadness, anger, happiness, love, remorse, forgiveness, etc. I consider this veil a training ground. We are supposed to learn things here. I often am asked, "What are we supposed to learn?" and "What is the meaning of life?" If I had the answer to that question, I would be the all-powerful and all-knowing. I do know, however, that we have to keep learning. We can't settle or be stuck regardless of how hard it is. One lesson I personally believe we are supposed to learn here is how to live a life of balance: how to be compassionate, selfless, kind, open, and—the hardest one—nonjudgmental. When you click through social media, you see judgment in almost every single post. We cannot control others, but we can certainly control our reactions to their judgment.

Regarding veil two, let's say you go to visit Grandma in the hospital and she is very sick. You know that she will soon be crossing, and you would like to say goodbye (I say that there are never true good-byes), so you go to visit her. When you get to the hospital, she tells you that she sees her mother. You think Grandma has lost her mind and the Alzheimer's has set in. In actuality, she saw her mother.

Let me explain how that works. Everyone is crossed in by someone he or she knows; it does not have to be an immediate family member, but for the sake of the example, we will say it is her mother who is coming to cross her over. It is important that you understand what is going on at that moment. This is the moment when Grandma understands that there is nothing to fear about crossing. If Grandma is nonverbal, you will notice she will look to either the right or left corner or right above her head, indicating the time for you to say what you think you need to say to make you feel complete before she crosses.

If Grandma is an Alzheimer's or dementia patient, I want to explain a few things to you. I am *not* a doctor or a higher power, but I do get to speak to thousands of your people after they have arrived into veil two, so I can only refer to my experience.

I waited over seven years to write this book to research and gain experiences to ensure there is consistency in the information a loved one who passes gives me. Many times we go to see loved ones who have Alzheimer's, and when they don't recognize us, we feel hurt or angry.

Please allow me to tell you what they tell me. They know exactly who you are and how you are related. They remember the chicken soup recipe they used to make when you were a child. So why when you walk in the room do they appear to not know who you are?

Think of the diseased part of the brain like a filter that is full of gunk and debris. You walk in the room. They make eye contact with you. They know you are their granddaughter, and they want to say your name. Somewhere there is a disconnect between knowing it is you and what comes out of their mouths. When the thought of you hits the dirty filter, it gets lost in translation. Unfortunately, this situation can make the person agitated and angry. Their anger can sometimes trigger your anger at them for being edgy, and then you have a big, angry, stressful mess.

It is so important that you understand that they want to say your name, but the filtered part of the brain won't let them. So yes, Grandma does remember the necklace you are wearing and the pearls she gave you. She just can't get it out. When I work with hospice patients and their families, I always tell the loved ones to continue to talk to them as though they are not asking you who you are. Tell them you watered their flowers or got their mail like they once asked you to do. I promise you 100 percent that you will see their agitation stop. It's so important that you understand that somewhere in the broken part of the brain, they in fact do know who you are. *They have encouraged me to add this to the book so you can have a better understanding of how their brain works during this stressful time.*

When your people cross into veil two they *all* describe it to me in three ways.

1. It is warm, like being in the sun without sunburn.
2. They are light. Now when I was a teenager first talking to your people and learning to accept all of this, I thought light meant flying or floating. No, light means no stress, no worry, no concern for health, no feeling jaded or angry. I can relate this most to you by the days you have when you just can't get out of bed. You think at the end of the day that you have no idea how you made it through the day. That is an example of a heavy day. Your people are light.
3. For the sake of the conversation, take happy and healthy along with peaceful, tranquil, calm, and free, and put that in a little ball and tie a pretty bow around it. Jack it up on steroids about ten thousand times, and that is where your people stay. I call it Happyville. Now this book could go on for days if we talked religion, so Happyville is a word I like to use since it pretty much sums up where they are.

How many times have you felt like you just can't forget or drop something? How about when people cross over? Have you or someone you loved came close to crossing over? There are so many more scenarios we have that we just get stuck. We ruminate on them over and over.

I will share a personal story that perhaps will help you understand the term *move on* or *move forward*.

In August of 2014, my son was a recent graduate and starting college in just a few short weeks. A week before classes were to start, I got a text at 3:00 a.m. but had the ringer off. The text read, "I'm sorry, Mom." I got the text at 7:00 a.m. on a weekend, when I usually sleep till 9:00 or 10:00 a.m. My guide must have woken me to spring into action. I ran to his room, where he was barely breathing and on the floor. I immediately called for my husband to come and help me revive or bring him back to consciousness. I went into business mode and called 911 to send an ambulance. The ambulance arrived and the paramedics asked me what had happened. I had no idea other than he had sent me a text saying he was sorry. I came downstairs to find six medicine bottles empty on the counter in a line. They took the bottles and loaded him up to go to the hospital right away. When I arrived at the hospital, he was in the emergency room being evaluated. They took him straight to the ICU for thirty-six hours to make sure he was stable enough to transport to a facility to help him deal with what was going on emotionally. He was unconscious when I left that evening. When my best friend Kim and I arrived the next day, he was still very high and talking to one of the social workers there. When we arrived and I hugged him, he was very distant. He said, "I am going to do this again, but next time I will be successful." This statement is something he does not remember saying to us but something that remains in the back of my head every day. On day four he seemed to have all of the medication out of his system and was ready to come home. They advised us to wait a few more days so he could stabilize some. On that Friday we bought a safe for the medication and made sure that when he came home he felt "normal." We brought him home, where he felt as though my paranoia and concern were annoying and unwarranted. He asked me to stop checking on him and said he was fine. He continued medication and treatment for six more months. He is now off of medication and therapy altogether.

I am still concerned and worried about his statement that he would try again and be successful. I focus every day on sending out positive vibes and thoughts to the universe that my child is moving forward, is strong and brave, and knows to ask for help if he ever feels like that again. How can a mother move on and not worry about having to find her child has cross over? The "moving on" is not always an easy thing to do, but I will share some tips on what I have done to allow me that small bit of freedom.

The first question is probably, "How did you not know if you are intuitive?" I have found that other than small things like taking a different road or not doing something because my guide tells me not to, I can't read for myself or family. I have spoken to other intuitive people like myself who state the same thing. I think the reason you can't read for yourself or close family is because you are still suppose to live and experience things like everyone else. It sucks to be honest, and to think that if it happened again that I would not be aware of it is quite scary.

How have I managed to move on or keep living? While he was in the hospital, I kept busy and still met with people who were in crisis and needed help. Some people say I was very strong to help others while my son was in the hospital. He is still my son, and kids don't always listen to their parents or what they have to say. This is no different with someone who is intuitive. At no point is he or my daughter walking around hanging on and listening to my every word. I don't look at that as being strong though. I was put here to help other people get through tough times or times they think they can't make it through. Clearly with some of the past situations I have experienced, it allows me to be able to relate to the people I have helped and will continue to help. Some life lessons are less than pleasurable and downright shitty.

I would be lying to you if I didn't say there is a little part of me that worries about the situation daily. The difference is there is a place for it. Many people who can't move on or get stuck will think about it all day long and create stories and scenarios. The guilt sets in and controls your daily routine. (I should have ... I could have ... Why didn't I ...?) As a mother, I made the best effort to make sure he had good doctors, a comfortable house, and caring family. The one thing I can't do is make him do anything. He is a twenty-year-old man who has to make decisions for himself. If anyone is a parent then you know this is one the hardest lessons you must learn. If you allow yourself a few minutes each day or week to feel sad, worried, concerned, out of control, or just a mess then you will be able to proceed with the rest of the day or week. At no point can someone tell you how to grieve or how long to grieve. The biggest concern I have is people who can't move on at all. You worrying about a situation or person does *not* stop what is going to happen. This sounds so much easier than it is to actually do, but I will give you some tips that I personally use to help with that.

Let's assume for the moment that your loved one was not as lucky and has crossed over into Happyville. You are empty, sad, and alone. Your guilt is uncontrollable, and you think constantly about how you could have stopped or changed the outcome. You think about all of the amazing things that person will not have an opportunity to see and experience with you. That alone is enough to make you never want to leave your bed, let alone talk to anyone. The fun things you guys used to do and laugh about are no longer an option ... or are they? Of course, your person isn't here any longer in human form. You cannot call or hug him or her. You can, however, laugh, walk, and experience great joy with him or her. No, I have not lost my mind. Let me explain. As mentioned earlier, when people cross into Happyville, they are not lost forever. They get to visit and experience all of the amazing things you guys experienced together. If you are lost in grief for a prolonged period of time, you will not see the signs your lost loved ones send you to let you know they are right there! They love the wooded areas and mountains, so plan a trip for a hike with your brother who crossed and talk about things that are going on that you need him for. Talk to your loved one about an annoying coworker or spouse who is on your last nerve. It isn't so much about moving on as it is about learning the new normal. Grandma loved baking cookies with you on Thanksgiving, so get yourself the recipe and turn on the music you listened to and make the cookies with her. Talk out loud. Better yet, laugh out loud when you drop the flour on the floor. I will mention again that just because you do those activities and talk out loud does not mean she will come on demand. It is very healthy, though, and cathartic to do the activities you did together. Many times you want to avoid the situations you once did together because it is too painful to experience alone without that person. Please remember that that person isn't gone forever, never to be heard from again.

Now let me address some items and make needed corrections to what most people believe. Let's go back to Grandma for a minute. Grandma and Grandpa were the glue to the family. They would host holidays, and all the family would visit from all over and spend amazing holidays as a loving family. Now that Grandma and Grandpa have crossed over and are dancing under the moon together, you decide that you are banning Christmas and never putting up another tree in your life because you would never be able to do it the same way. I'm going to burst you bubble now. First of all, Grandma will see Grandpa, yes, but together forever under the moon ... sorry, it doesn't work that way. Happyville is like Woodstock—one big, happy place where you feel the same way about everyone. I know you want to believe that your sister and mother and grandfather are all there together watching over you and comparing notes. They may visit you but not usually together, and they are not comparing notes—sorry. Banning Christmas is not going to help honor her memory or show them that you can have the holidays without them. Go out to the tree farm, pick out a nice tree, have Christmas, and start a new tradition. You are allowed to hurt for as long as you hurt. What you are not allowed to do is to get stuck in hurt. Getting stuck seriously only affects you. Often people are sad that their people are not all together as one big happy family, but again, you are reading this book in veil one where we have an assortment of emotions. In veil two there is not an assortment of emotions—only one. I can't put into words the euphoria they experience and honestly can't imagine that on a constant basis, but wow, it sounds amazing.

When we are here in veil one, we are very close with our family and friends. We protect our family and want to make sure they are well taken care of after we cross. We write a will to make sure the family house goes to our kids and the cars get to the grandkids. We make sure every I is dotted and T is crossed. Now we have crossed to veil two, so none of those things are a concern to us. Not to make it sound like we don't care anymore, but when it comes to material things, nothing does matter.

I spoke to a sweet old lady who came through a few years ago in a private reading for her granddaughter, and I learned a whole lot from her. She stayed much longer than normal, and she made it very clear that they don't care if you sell the family home or auction the cars. It seriously doesn't matter to them.

It is always hilarious to me—and by hilarious, I mean

ridiculous—when I hear someone say, "Mom would be rolling over in her grave." No, she would not! Someone started saying that to make someone else feel bad about not acting particular way. I don't care if the farm was in the family for three hundred years—if you don't need it, sell it. This isn't going to bring Grandma back to haunt you. The same goes for you not getting to see her before she crossed. So many people I see are really hurt and stressed by that. Just so you know, Grandma is around you and sees you, so if you didn't say bye (no reason to—she is only going to veil two), then just start the new relationship now. I know that sounds really weird and strange, but you really do start a new relationship with your people. Once you know how they come around (more on that later), then it makes it really easy to be able to have that new relationship.

If you have ever done tai chi or other energy-balancing work, you know you work with the energies around you and hone them in to make the chi ball. This would be all the energies you gather in one big ball.

So when we cross, that is basically what happens to us in veil two. We are energy particles. There is no special town where we run into Bill from down the street and see that he now has hair and looks great. That said, when people come through to me, they come through in human form. Yes, I see them in full person form. This makes for fun trips to the grocery store or mall where there are lots of people! I try to stay away from large groups of people unless I am doing an appearance or a party. If a room has twenty people in it to the naked eye, for me it can be many more. I see them just like I do you except they are translucent. I see Grandma wearing her favorite sweater or gardening gloves, only I can see whatever is behind that as well.

Another interesting thing I have learned over the many years of chatting and meeting your awesome people is that if they have crossed young, they don't know the energy to appear older. If someone was twenty-five when he or she crossed, he or she will not be fifty if he or she is visiting me when you are here; he or she does not have that energy and does not understand that energy to appear to me in that way. I use the example of a cousin crossing at twenty-five years of age, and the parents coming to visit me ten years later. When the cousin comes through, he wouldn't be thirty-fie. He would still look around twenty to me. That said, if Grandma was ninety-seven when she crossed, she can come through looking younger. This doesn't mean she will come at seventeen or twenty. It means she can come around fifty or sixty.

I have learned a lot of interesting things about our energy as we get older. Jack Lalanne was old but healthy when he crossed, so I would assume he could come back at ninety comfortably. That is not the case ... It seems as though once we get to about seventy-two or so, our energy dissipates. It doesn't leave, but our vibration is much lighter, making it a lot more difficult for our energy to visit at that older age.

Oh, how they love to be validated! I have had many clients who have sat on my couch or been in a group and connected with the person right away. This seems easy enough. "Oh, it's my mother," so you would think she would go on to whatever she has to talk about or ask her. Sometimes, but usually it's more validity stuff. I used to quilt, I made special soup, I planted only this flower, etc.

While I enjoy talking to them, sometimes they tend to blab on and on. Yes, it's a regular conversation! There is no, "I am sorry," "I miss you," or "I love you" in the conversation. Let's remember Happyville and the fact that they no longer have the capacity to feel that anxiety or stress of missing you or being sorry. The love part goes without saying. They want to talk about the pictures or the house. They want to talk about the grandkids and let you know exactly what has been going on in your house. As a person people look to for this kind of guidance, I love it! They are not vague and pretty much like to tell you things that only they would know or the family would know. I always recommend people to take notes since they can yammer on for a good bit of time while they are here chatting. They will say they are with you all the time, but as mentioned before, there is no time where they are, so no, they are not with you all the time.

I have had the question, "If they are not sorry and do not miss me, then why do they visit?" Just remember, they visit for you, not them. They are pretty intelligent and can see what is going on; they just aren't going to stress about it like you would. They aren't going to stress that you are fighting with your sister, but they will be around at times to try to give you guidance to end the fighting for your own benefit and sanity.

Sometimes there are people who come through who you may not recognize right away. I wish everyone would come and say, "I am her mom." It would make my life so much easier. Sometimes they come and tell me exactly who they are, and man, it is awesome for me to not have to do the validity thing for them. That can be draining and stressful. I always tell people that you don't always get what you want, but you do get what you need.

I will use the example of you coming to see me, and for weeks before your visit, you come and tell your Grandma to please come through. You wear her rings, carry her picture, and make sure to only see me on her birthday so it guarantees her coming through. Let's go back to the no time thing here for a second. She has no idea it is her birthday. She doesn't have a calendar, and she isn't looking at some watch thinking everyone should be celebrating her birthday. She will follow you to the first medium you see so she can talk to you. The rings and the photos once again are material things, and they don't care about material things at all. They may, however, bring them up if they are visiting. They often will show me the ring they are wearing pretty much down to the band and the stone and ask where the ring is. You may have it or your other family member may have it, but you should know what she is talking about at that moment. Once again, this is their fun way of being validated. They do not mention the ring because you wore it to see me. Grandma comes through, and you are happy. If Grandma doesn't show up and your first cousin who crossed from suicide comes through, then that is who you were supposed to see and talk to. I don't make the rules, and I have stopped trying to understand their reasoning other than I know for a fact that you get what you need.

At home you water the plants Granny gave you and talk to her all the time in your head. You tell her how you miss her and how she gave you this amazing plant, and you think of her daily. That is sweet, but she can't hear you. You have to talk out loud to her. They have made it clear for years that you have to talk out loud. I have no idea why this is so. I can't give you some amazing reason as to why. Don't get excited—just because you talk out loud doesn't mean that person is coming through. Sometimes you are talking to yourself, but if they are around you, they can hear you. They usually give you signs they are around. You are just looking for them to be the signs you see in the movies where they are big and exaggerated. No, they are subtle and can only be seen a few ways. (Refer to the FAQs.)

Veil three is where your spirit guides are. Why are

guides chosen, and are they related to you? No, they are never related to you, and as far as how guides are chosen, it remains a mystery to me. My daughter's guide is from Egypt and a woman from the 1200s. My guide is an American Indian who goes by the name Chief. My daughter can see my guide, but I can't see hers. Every generation is stronger than the generation before, so she gets to see others' guides while I cannot on a consistent basis. Your guide or guides are with you through your lifetime and are chosen prior to your birth.

Veil four is where your guardian angels are. Your guardian angels were never people, and you don't get your own guardian angel to carry around with you. When we cross, we will never get to veil four since the beings in veil four have never had a human soul. We all get to pull from the same group of guardian angels.

Veil five is your higher power. I won't delve into a big debate on religion, but I will say that for me, my higher power is God. I have several reasons as to why I believe in God and angels, but I feel as though for each of us that is a very personal connection we make.

Chapter 4

THE HUMAN CONNECTION AND LOSS
ALICE AND CHERYL

elow is a story that outlines the closeness of the human connection and devastation of loss. This story will help us segue into discussing grief and how we can absolutely continue forward.

"Alice," her mom called.

"Yeah, Mom, I'll be right down."

Alice and her mom had always been close. Her mom and dad divorced when she was a little girl. Her dad moved in with a woman he had been having an affair with throughout the whole marriage. Alice had depression and anxiety since she was a little girl. Her mom became her security blanket and made sure Alice got every ounce of love a person could get.

"Alice, I could not be more proud of you!" she squealed.

Alice was heading off to college but made sure to not stray too far from home. She was going to Towson University, which was only an hour and a half from her home on the Eastern Shore in Maryland.

"Thank you, Mom," she replied and gave her the biggest bear hug a person could give. "Mom, I don't know if I should go and leave you. I don't want you to be alone."

"Oh Alice, you are the beat of my heart, and I promise I will be just fine. We will talk every day," she assured her. They both teared up, and Alice told her mother that she was the reason she had made it this far. "Alice my dear, I love you more and more every day. You have turned into a young woman who makes me happy and proud with every thought."

There was a secret that Alice's mom, Cheryl, was keeping from her. She had gone to the doctor after not feeling very well, and they had given her an x-ray and found a small spot on her lung. She was due for additional tests in a few weeks, but the doctor alluded to the fact that it looked abnormal.

Cheryl never remarried after Alice's dad left and made Alice her number one priority. She most certainly did not want to mention this to Alice on the day she was heading off to college!

"Okay, Alice, I think everything is all loaded up. Don't forget Clover and Teddy," she added.

Clover and Teddy were both stuffed animals she'd had since she was a little girl and slept with every night.

"Mom, are you kidding me?" she replied. "I have them in my 'everything special' bag. I sprayed some of your perfume on them so I feel at home while I am gone."

More tears began, and Cheryl said, "We have got to go before you never, ever leave!" They snickered and hopped in the car.

After a ton of traffic and a brief stop to McDonald's, they finally arrived at Towson University. "Okay, Alice, let's find this dorm room and get you settled."

They came to the freshmen dorms that they visited earlier that year and found her roommate, Kimberly, who was there with her mom, Ellen, and was very nervous about being on her own. Cheryl could feel her emotions running high with the tests looming next week. She could only see her little Alice growing up and becoming a young woman. She excused herself and went to the restroom, where she proceeded to cry for a good five minutes, not because her daughter was growing up, but that she didn't want to leave this planet just yet. After finally getting herself together, she went back to the dorm, where Ellen had brought a nice TV for them to use and a lot of girly things that made the dorm a home. Kimberly and Alice were talking about a boy they saw moving into a different dorm house. Cheryl and Ellen laughed and talked about what kind of boy trouble the girls would get into.

"Well, little girl, it's time for you to get settled and time for me to leave before the traffic gets too bad."

"It's okay, Mom, you could stay here," said Alice.

"I think it's time for you to make your own mac and cheese tonight for a change."

"Mom, I don't think I can do this without you," said Alice.

"Come here, little girl, and give me a hug and count to ten." Cheryl would do this with Alice every time she felt anxiety. Alice ran to her mom and hugged her for a good five minutes and cried and cried. "Alice, I want you to take some deep breaths with me and count to ten." They did this together and held on for a few minutes longer. "Alice, you will be just fine, and I will call you the second I get home."

"I love you, Mom," Alice whimpered.

"I love you too, little girl."

On her way home, all Cheryl could do was think about how she wasn't ready to go yet and how Alice wasn't ready for her to go either. Somehow she got home in what seemed to be seconds. Her thoughts of her daughter without her had kept her mind so preoccupied that she didn't even realize she was driving. She got in and gave Alice a call right away.

"Hey there, little girl."

"Hi, Mom! I was really worried about you, but I am glad you made it home safe."

"How are you doing?" Cheryl asked.

"I'm doing good, Mom. I met my professor today while I was walking around campus."

"Which professor?" Cheryl asked.

"I met Professor Wheeler, my English professor. He is really funny and told me not to worry too much. He said as long as I did 100 percent perfect, I would pass his class." Alice and Cheryl both laughed.

"I guess you better study hard," said Cheryl. "Well, little girl, have a good night sleep, and I will chat with you in the morning."

"I love you, Mom," said Alice.

"Ugh, it's six thirty. You would think after forty years I would be used to getting up this early, but nope, I hate it as much now as I did twenty years ago. Coffee, give me coffee," said Cheryl to herself as she was trying to get motivated to get to the dreaded doctor's appointment. *Workout or no workout, hmm. I say I lay here for a few more minutes and snuggle the cat.* After a good thirty minutes of lounging, Cheryl managed to get herself together for the doctor. The phone began to ring, and Cheryl knew it was Alice.

"Hi, little girl!"

"Hi, Mom," said Alice. "I have my first class in fifteen minutes."

"Well, little girl, you will do wonderful. I have a few errands today, but let's talk tonight. Good luck!"

"Thanks, Mom. Love you."

Cheryl had a short drive to Anne Arundel Medical Center in Annapolis, where her first MRI and PET scan were scheduled. "Okay, think positive, think positive, think positive," said Cheryl to herself. "Hi, I am here to see Dr. George." Dr. George is an oncologist that her doctor referred her to and is listed as the top oncologist in Maryland.

"The office is busy, great," said Cheryl. She wasn't known for her patience, but she signed in and surfed Facebook and Instagram for a while.

"Ms. Ross, we will see you now."

Think positive, think positive, she thought again to herself.

"Hi, Cheryl," said Dr. George. "Is it okay if I call you Cheryl?"

"Yes, please do."

"Great, you can call me Jennifer or Jen. I like my patients to feel comfortable."

"Whew, okay. Jen sounds great," said Cheryl.

"I have all of your x-rays from Dr. Young, and he has concerns over a few spots on your lungs. We will do an MRI today and a PET scan. That will show us any hot spots or possible cancer spots. At that point we will decide if a biopsy is needed." Cheryl started to tear up and told Jen about her daughter and that she wasn't ready to go yet. "Cheryl, let's not put the cart before the horse," said Dr. Jen. "If in fact you do have cancer, there are so many amazing treatments that it is not considered a death sentence if you catch it early. Let's get these tests done and get you on the road to mending, whatever you may or may not have."

Cheryl felt so much better about these tests thanks to Dr. Jen. The first test was the PET scan. While lying on the table she thought of Alice when she was a young teenager and them playing with water balloons. This made her laugh, and the tech asked her to please stay still. She thought, *The guy must think I'm crazy to be laughing during a PET scan.* She thought of Alice's best friend Debra surprising her on her sixteenth birthday with balloons and a whipped cream pie to the face and again started to laugh. "Ma'am, please stay still. The faster I can get this completed, the faster you will be out of here."

When they were finally through with that test, they wanted the MRI with contrast, so she sat down and got an IV for the contrast. *I hate needles,* Cheryl thought, *but I am ready to be out of this place. I hate it here already.* This test seemed pretty quick other than the loud noises the MRI made, and they made it very clear that if she moved they would have to start all over. Dr. Jen told Cheryl that she would see her in a few days when all of the tests came back. She told her not to worry but go for a nice walk while the weather was still nice.

That night Cheryl felt all alone and empty without her little girl Alice. Like clockwork the phone rang, and it was Alice. "Hi, Mom!" She sounded very excited.

"Wow, little girl, I guess the day went good?" asked Cheryl.

"Mom I had the best day ever! Kimberly and I get

along really well, and her brother is supposed to come this weekend and show us around. Kimberly's brother graduated a few years ago and knows the campus and area really well."

"Oh, little girl, I am so happy the day went well for you."

"How was your day, Mom?"

Knowing that she wasn't going to tell her the non-amazing day she had, she said, "Good, cleaned up around here and got a pedicure." Cheryl felt bad about lying but didn't want to alarm her.

"Good, if anyone deserves it, for sure it's you."

"Thank you, little girl. I love you."

"Love you too, Mom."

Cheryl had told no one about her spots—not her sister, and her best friend had moved away to Australia a few years ago with her husband, so she pretty much kept to herself or with Alice. *I have got to get a life and meet someone*, thought Cheryl. *I think I will go to the animal shelter and volunteer tomorrow.*

"Hi, Shannon," said Cheryl when she arrived at the shelter. "I have so many towels and sheets for the pups today."

After about three trips, she was ready to walk the dogs. She met an amazing pup named Sassy that had terminal cancer, and she decided, *That is who I am walking first.* On her walk she decided that Sassy was going to be the one to hear about her spots.

"Sassy girl, I might have what you have. I don't know what to do," said Cheryl. She sat down on the bench and cried. Sassy jumped up and licked her face as if to say it was okay. That second she knew that Sassy wasn't staying in that shelter one more day. Almost running back, she flung open the door and asked for Michele, the adoption coordinator.

"Michele, I am taking Sassy. I need her with me." Michele was elated and of course they knew her home was a good one, so the papers were filled and Sassy was on her way to her new home!

At 6:30 the phone was ringing like clockwork. "Hi, little girl!"

"Mom, are you okay? You sound out of breath."

Laughing, Cheryl said, "That is because the cat was trying to attack the dog."

"Mom, what dog?" asked Alice.

"Oh, I adopted a dog named Sassy today that has terminal cancer in her lung. It might be like mine," she said without thinking.

"What?" Silence on both ends of the phone. "Mom! Mom! What did you just say! Did you just tell me you have cancer!"

With no way of getting around what had just come out of her mouth, Cheryl was forced to tell the truth. "Alice, I don't want you to be alarmed."

"Don't be alarmed! Mom, you just told me you have terminal cancer!"

"Alice …"

"Don't Alice me, Mom! Why would you not tell me? I am coming home!"

"Alice, please listen to me!" pleaded Cheryl. All she could hear were sobs on the other end of the phone.

Kimberly said, "Ms. Ross, what is going on? Alice can barely breathe."

"Kimberly, I told her I may have cancer and she thinks it's terminal and I can't even get a word in now."

Kimberly managed to calm Alice enough to listen to her mother. "Alice, please listen to me. I had an x-ray done a few weeks ago, and they found a few spots so they sent me to an oncologist to get a few more tests done to see if it is in fact cancer. I didn't want to tell you till I knew for sure if it was something. Alice? Alice, are you there?"

"Yes, Mom, I am here," whimpered Alice.

"Little girl, I should know something in the next few days, but I really want you to try and not think—"

"Not think about what, Mom! The fact the only person I have may die! Alice said angrily. *"I can't believe you didn't tell me!"*

"Alice, I know you're angry, but—"

"I can't talk to you right now!" Alice hung up.

Cheryl grabbed Sassy and just held her, feeling sad, scared, and all alone. A few minutes later the phone rang, and it was Alice. "Mom, I am sorry I hung up on you, but I am scared you're going to die," cried Alice.

"Oh little girl, please let's wait for the tests to come back, and I promise you I won't keep you in the dark ever again. I was trying to not distract you," Cheryl said.

"I love you, Mom to the moon and back."

"I love you too, little girl, to the moon and back."

Monday rolled around, and the big day to see Dr. Jen was here. "Ugh, I guess I've got to face the day," she said to Sassy. Sassy started to growl and bark. "Sassy girl, what is wrong with you?" Just then Alice jumped in the bed. "Little girl! What are you doing here? How did you get here?"

"Mom, I only had to turn in a few papers over the Internet today and I did them last night, so I am all yours today!"

Cheryl grabbed her and hugged her and began to cry. "Mom, it's okay. You took care of me all of my life. It's my turn now," said Alice.

"I still don't know how you got home. Why do I smell bacon? I know you can't cook your way out of a paper bag." Just then she heard that familiar voice.

"Hi Ms. R!"

"Hey, trouble, what in the world are you doing here?" she asked, laughing.

"Alice called me yesterday about those little spots, and I told her that you were just really a cheetah inside and that is why you had spots." They all laughed. "Ms. R, you are like my mom too, so I picked her up this morning at five thirty, and here we are. I made you breakfast, so get up now!" Debra barked.

"Okay, girls, here we are." They arrived at AAMC and went straight to Dr. Jen.

"Hi there, Cheryl. I see you have company with you today."

"I do! This is my daughter Alice and her best friend Debra, my other daughter."

"Well I am glad you have a good support system, which is always the key to any healing that is needed," said Dr. Jen.

"Well, Doctor, how do I look?" asked Cheryl.

"Well, I did get the tests back, and I believe you do have an early stage of lung cancer." Alice broke into tears and held Debra tight. "Girls, please let me finish so you can understand the treatment and prognosis. We did some blood work while your mom was here last week, and it doesn't look like it hasn't spread anywhere else, so I think our treatment option is very straightforward."

"Okay, Dr. Jen, where do we begin?" Cheryl asked, choking back tears.

"I think we do eight rounds of chemo and then see if you will need radiation. You are in the early stages, so the prognosis is actually very good." There was silence in the room while Cheryl looked at the doctor with a deer in the headlights silence. "Cheryl, this is wonderful that you were able to get to me early. I feel really good about this treatment. Alice, the best thing that you can do right now is go back to school and—"

"*No! I am not leaving my mom to deal with this alone! I will figure something out, but I will be here with her every step of the way,*" cried Alice.

"We will begin treatment on Thursday and there will be a few days after chemo that will not be fun for you, but I think if you follow my orders, you will get through this fine."

"Will I lose my hair?" asked Cheryl.

"Maybe, but if you do, it will grow back after you stop your treatment. You will come every other week for eight treatments and midway we will do another PET scan to see how the tumors are looking."

"Okay, Dr. Jen, I am ready to kick this stupid cancer in the ass!"

"Mom!" Alice said, laughing. "You never cuss."

"I think if I am fighting cancer I get a big pass to cuss." They all laughed, even Dr. Jen.

Alice and Cheryl drove back to Towson to talk to the advisors. Debra said she would help take care of the animals and with some of the cooking since Alice could *not* cook. Alice went to Professor Wheeler and explained her mom's situation and then went to the advisor while Cheryl packed up her stuff with Kimberly.

"Ms. R, I will be down to visit with my mom on Thanksgiving break," said Kimberly.

"You know you don't have to do that, right?"

"Not asking permission—I am telling you what we are doing," said Kimberly.

"Yes ma'am. I am so happy you and Alice have become close so fast."

"So given the situation, Mom, they are letting me do my classes online except biology. I can take that next semester. Professor Wheeler said that I can do his class online and if there were any questions he couldn't answer by e-mail that he would Skype me. So see, I am just fine to be there with you," said Alice.

"Well, I am very blessed to have you and your amazing support system in my corner."

"If you are going to kick cancer's ass, Mom, you need me too." Laughter once again ensued, and they soon discovered laughter indeed is the best medicine.

The alarm rang promptly at 6:30 a.m. like it always had. Alice slept in bed with Cheryl after a marathon of *Orange Is the New Black* on Netflix the night before. "Mom, can you please turn that God awful thing off?" grumbled Alice.

"Little girl, we have to be at Dr. Jen's at eight o'clock this morning. Where is that Debra when you need a good breakfast?" Cheryl said, laughing.

"Can we just hit Dunkin this morning, Mom, please. I need some serious caffeine."

"Sounds like a great plan."

"I think we should take some games or something. Dr. Jen said the treatments last about four to five hours.

I'll grab the cards and take out Sassy. Then I'll meet you in the car, Mom."

"Good morning, Ms. Ross, how are you today?" the receptionist asked.

"Well, I am here, so I will say not all that great." They smiled, and Cheryl and Alice sat down nervously.

"Ms. Ross, come on back, and we will get you all set." As they both walked back, Alice grabbed her mother's hand.

"My name is Kristin, and I will be your treatment nurse for the entire time you are here. We will get to know each other pretty well over the next few months."

"Well, Kristen, call me Cheryl, and feel free to do anything possible to get my mind off of this. Kristin, this is Alice, my daughter."

"Hi, Kristin. I plan on being here as much as I can."

"Alice, feel free to go to the mall or roam around from time to time while she is getting her treatments. Sometimes it can be a little draining."

"I plan on sitting right here with my mom," Alice said sternly.

"Okay, Cheryl, there are three steps in this particular chemo plan. After a few treatments, Dr. George will check to make sure this is the plan that works the best for you. I will give you an IV and then some basic nausea meds first, then two different types of chemo in intervals. Should take about four hours or so."

"I hate needles, just so you know," said Cheryl.

"Oh my friend, you will get used to them soon enough," said Kristin. "Are you ready for the IV?"

"Um, not really, but I guess so."

"Okay, you will feel a little prick and then a bit of burning after I flush it. You will then feel a cooling sensation with the nausea medication. If you have any questions along the way, just let me know."

"Ouch," said Cheryl.

"Mom, stop being a baby please," Alice said, laughing.

"Okay, Cheryl, you are well on your way to recovery."

Cheryl and Alice talked about all kinds of things during the four hours. They played five hundred rummy at least three times, and Alice showed her a picture of the cute boy she had met at Towson.

"Okay, Cheryl, you are all finished today! One down and seven more to go. Today you should feel okay, but tomorrow and the next day you may feel very crummy and may vomit some. This is all very normal as your body recovers from the chemo. I will see you in two weeks, but if anything arises, call Dr. George or myself without hesitation. I am giving you blood work orders as well to get your blood drawn before your next treatment."

"Why does she need that?" asked Alice.

"Chemo can sometimes lower your blood platelets, so it's our benchmark to make sure her body is strong enough for the next treatment. Nothing more than preliminary routine things we do," said Kristin.

That night Debra came over and cooked a nice meal

for all three of them. Alice kept asking over and over again how Cheryl was feeling. "Oh, little girl, stop worrying about me. I will tell you ASAP if I need anything. If you want we can watch another episode of *Orange Is the New Black* and snuggle up in bed."

"Sounds great, I'll grab the popcorn."

"Mom? Mom? Hey, Mom, turn off that stupid alarm. *Mom*!"

"Why are you yelling!"

"Turn off the alarm!"

"Oh my, I feel really crappy and tired. I didn't even hear it go off this morning. I think I want to sleep a little bit longer."

"Okay, I have some things I have to do for school, and Professor Wheeler is Skyping me at seven thirty about a thesis I need to do. I will make breakfast after if you are hungry."

"I'm not in the mood for anything at all, blah. Maybe some applesauce or something, but I want to sleep more first."

At 10:45 a.m. Cheryl finally got out of bed but only to get sick and then go back to bed. "I think I need some ginger ale and crackers," said Cheryl.

"I already have my arsenal of stuff here, Mom, so go get in bed and I will bring you something."

For the next two days this seemed to be the pattern. Thursday morning rolled around, and at 6:30 Cheryl woke up even though the alarm did not go off. It was a new day, and she felt like her old self again. She woke up Alice, and off they went for a short but nice walk outside.

"Alice, you do know I am going to beat this, right?"

"Mom, if anyone can do it, it will be you for sure. You are the strongest woman I know on this planet. You are my world, Mom. When that asshole of a father left us, if I didn't have you who knows what would have happened? He had the nerve to try to call me last week to call me and ask about you! I think Debra's father saw him somewhere and told him what was going on. I told him that if he cared enough, he wouldn't have left us for that whore."

"Alice, you can't hold that grudge against him. You don't have to like him, but if you are negative when you think about him, you let him control you. You are hurt that your father—"

"*Stop* calling him that," said Alice.

"You are hurt that your person who donated to make you wasn't there for you. You have every right to be. I just want you to work through that in your own way. Don't worry about him anyway, little girl. We are a dynamic duo."

"I love you to the moon and back, Mom."

"Ditto," said Cheryl.

"Ms. Ross?"

"That is me."

"Come back with me. I have to get some blood work before your appointment upstairs."

"Ugh, okay, fine."

"Mom, stop being a baby!" Alice said, laughing.

"All looks good with your blood work, so upstairs you go."

"Hey there Cheryl, Alice."

"Hi, Kristin," they said un unison.

"Wow, you girls are like two peas in a pod, aren't you?"

They all laughed. "I took a picture of my chickens to show you, Cheryl, to cheer you up some. I have pet chickens, and I call them my girls."

"Oh Mom, let's get a chicken," said Alice.

"Little girl, we need to get me through this, and I doubt Sassy would like that right now."

"Okay, Cheryl, you know the drill. Here comes the IV."

"Ouch!"

"Excuse her, Kristin, my mother is a two-year-old."

"It does hurt," Cheryl said, laughing.

This trip Alice brought a giant album of pictures from home so the two of them could do some scrapbooking to pass some time. Cheryl decided that instead of that she wanted to become a better cook and entertain when she was finished the chemo for good, so Kristin brought her tons of magazines. For four hours Cheryl ripped out recipes and home decor. Alice did her homework and fetched snacks for the both of them.

"Hello, Cheryl."

"Hi, Dr. Jen!"

"You look pretty good. How are you feeling? Are you getting sick in between treatments?"

"Only the first few days after the treatments, but other than that, Alice and I go for walks and a little light shopping."

"Well, fantastic. I will see you on Friday for your next PET scan. We will be able to tell how the treatments are working."

"I will have her there at eight a.m. sharp," said Alice.

Over the next few days, Cheryl lived on her normal ginger ale and cracker diet. She felt more tired than usual but assumed this was from more treatments. Alice was able to get a lot of work done, and Kimberly paid a visit on Wednesday to watch the new episode of *Orange Is the New Black*. All three girls sat in Cheryl's bed and watched and talked to the TV. Kimberly had bought a giant package of saltines from Sam's Club and also gave her a gift certificate for a pedicure. She said she didn't want her to have ugly feet.

"Ready, Mom? Time to see how the treatments are working. I am thinking positive, so let's get there."

On the way, they stopped by Dunkin Donuts and grabbed coffee. Cheryl started to get sick, so they pulled over. Dr. Jen had warned them that sometimes things you like you start to dislike while on chemo. Once they got to AAMC to the imaging department, Cheryl got a big orange juice and felt much better.

"Okay, Ms. Ross, it's time for the PET scan. Do you think this time you can stay still and not laugh?" asked the tech.

Giggling, Cheryl replied, "I think I can do that. I want it over fast this time."

She made it through the test without laughing. Her thoughts became sad again while worrying she would not be here to see her daughter get married or graduate. She quickly snapped out of that when Alice came in and asked the tech how it looked. The tech replied that he wasn't able to give the results of the tests and that all he did was perform them. Alice rolled her eyes and sucked her teeth.

Under her breath to her mom she said, "What an ass. You know he can read it."

"Alice, stop," Cheryl said, giggling.

"I am just saying, Mom, you know his ass knows how to read a test that he does all the time. He knows if something looks good or bad."

"Alice, I think he is cute, don't you?"

"Eww, Mom ... no I don't. I don't want to date someone that is lying to me about reading a test!"

"Alice honey, that is you protecting yourself. Not every man is going to be like your donor."

"I never said that, Mom!" snapped Alice.

"Little girl, you didn't have to. You are still hurt by your donor, and you feel untrusting, which is normal. Not everyone is like him, you know? I still say the tech is cute," Cheryl said, laughing.

"His name is Jean, Mom. Really? That is what I am wearing right now! Jeans. I am not dating a guy with a name of something I wear! I guess next you will want me to date shirt or sweater." They busted out laughing just as Jean the tech walked back in. "I swear he must think we are all a few floors short in the head ..."

"I don't know why I am so stressed about seeing Dr. Jen today."

"Mom, it's because its kind of big deal."

Cheryl and Alice both knew that it really was a big deal. They were going to find out if this chemo was working or if things had gotten worse. They both went in to Dr. Jen's office to wait. Dr. Jen was married with two kids, a cat, and a dog. It made Cheryl happy to know she was a mom too and would be gentle with her if it was really bad news. She liked football, which was a plus, but she was a Steelers' fan, which made Alice less of a fan of hers. She was a Bengals' fan, and her mother was a Ravens' fan.

"Mom, seriously, of all the doctors on the planet you pick one with bad taste in football." They laughed as Dr. Jen was walking in.

"Hi there, ladies. It appears I am walking in at a good time."

"Dr. Jen we are not Steelers' fans." They all laughed. "Alice says I have to go to a different doctor now." Alice spewed her water as she was drinking when her mom said that.

"Well, Alice, hopefully after my report you may change your mind."

"Really? What does that mean?" Alice asked eagerly.

"Well, Cheryl, you are responding better than any of us could have imagined! I think after your treatments, if this continues you may be cancer free. No promises, but it looks great."

Alice flung from the chair and hugged Dr. Jen, knocking her back in the chair. "Oh my, I am so sorry," said Alice.

"Dr. Jen, thank you so much," said Cheryl.

"I am ordering you Steelers' bedsheets the second I get home!" shrieked Alice. "I am suddenly a Steelers' fan!" They all laughed.

Over the next several weeks, it was business as usual. Go to chemo, cut out recipes and home decor. Alice did homework and grabbed snacks. They would home and do well the first night and then have two or three days of misery. Cheryl's hair was thinning but not all gone. She did start wearing a beanie though since she was a bit self-conscious. Her weight dropped from 140 to 113 by the time of the last visit.

"Mom, you are so skinny! We need to feed you after tomorrow's treatment. Let's go get a big dinner or something to celebrate the last treatment," said Alice.

"I tell you what—let's plan a trip somewhere to the beach. It's warm now, and I think we both deserve a beach trip. We can save up money, and when you are finished with finals, we can go to the beach. How does that sound to you?" asked Cheryl.

"Let's do it! I think we should go somewhere other than Ocean City. How about Outer Banks or something?"

"Little girl, that sounds amazing. Alice, you always drive me to the appointments. How about today I drive and you ride in the passenger seat for a change?"

"Mom, do you feel up to it?"

"Little girl, I am fine, and after this treatment I will be fit as a fiddle and ready to travel all around the globe."

"All right, Mom, if you say so. I will go get the travel magazine I picked up and bring it so we can do some planning."

"Why is traffic always so bad on Route 50?" asked Alice.

"Little girl, you have lived here nineteen years. You would think you would know how bad it gets by now."

This morning it was foggy with a bit of drizzle. They both hated the fog. Alice saw the movie *The Fog* by Stephen King and hated fog ever since. The traffic was so bad this morning they would be about thirty minutes late for the appointment. *But who cares, it's the last one!* thought Cheryl.

"It's kind of cool, Alice. You can barely see the top of the Bay Bridge. Look at it, Alice. It's like we are over the clouds like a rainbow or something. It's really rather majestic."

At that moment, there was a massive bang, and the car spun out of control. The bridge had two-way traffic that morning and the oncoming car veered into Cheryl's lane hitting her car head on. *"Mom, Mom, Mom …"*

The next thing Alice knew, she was on the ground on the bridge on a flat, hard stretcher board and was not able to move her neck. They didn't want her to in case of neck injuries. "Where is my mom? *How is my mom? She has cancer and we have to get to the hospital.*"

"Alice, she has been flown to John Hopkins, and I have no other info."

"Is she okay? I need to see her!"

"Alice, I need you to calm down. Your blood pressure is through the roof, and we are getting you to AAMC."

"I want to go where my mom is!" The sedative they gave her started to work, and she drifted off to sleep.

Cheryl came to in the helicopter and asked for Alice. "Where is my daughter? *Where is Alice?*"

"Cheryl, I need you to remain calm. Your daughter is going to be okay, and she is on her way to AAMC."

"Why am I in a helicopter?"

"You have severe injuries and some internal bleeding. We have to make sure to get you to Hopkins and get all of that under control."

"Please don't let anything happen to me. I am beating cancer, and I have to be here for my little girl."

The helicopter techs went into panic mode as Cheryl's pressure began to drop rapidly. "Cheryl, I need you to stay with us. I can see the hospital within our sight."

"Please don't let me go, not now. I can't go!" screamed Cheryl.

"Cheryl, can you hear us?"

"Yes, I can hear you! Dad, tell them I can hear them."

"She isn't responding. Grab the paddles."

"Dad," yelled Cheryl, "please tell them I can hear them! Dad, how are you here with me? Dad, tell them I am okay! I have to be okay! Alice needs me! Your grand-daughter needs me! Dad, is that me? Why can I see myself? How is that possible? Oh no, I can't go! Please, Dad, not yet!"

The techs lost Cheryl's heartbeat. The lead tech called the time of death at 9:04 a.m.

Chapter 5

MOVING ON

In the story of Cheryl and Alice, Alice is now forced to deal with the unexpected loss of her mother. Her mother was her anchor, her experience in life, and the most important thing she cared about.

This situation is not unusual. I talk to so many people who are often left in the same situation: parents losing kids, kids losing parents, siblings losing brothers and sisters, and world tragedy. Many people feel as though they will never be able to move forward with their lives, that the grief is all consuming. It is common for people get stuck in one dimension of the grief process.

The biggest problem people have is moving on after someone has crossed. The most challenging obstacle people face after someone has crossed is to move on, to take a step forward—putting one foot in front of the other in search of peace and comfort about what transpired.

I find that most of the time when a loved one moves on, he/she is still stuck in the sadness and loneliness. The new normal is difficult to accept as there are constant reminders—holidays, routines, traditions, birthdays, and even just the simple things. People are sad, empty, guilty, and lost.

These feelings are important as they are all part of the five levels of the grieving process. To move forward, all five stages must be addressed. Sometimes even after people have allowed themselves to work through all five levels, they are still at a dead-end road about how to move forward.

The following stages of grief are listed in the most common order. It's important to note that people may experience them in a different order. There are many times people will bounce back and forth between the stages before you settle in to acceptance.

Denial/Shock: "I can't believe she/he is gone." You want to deny the event ever happened. You want to go to sleep and wake up like it was a bad dream. Shock is mostly a factor with an untimely passing. It can leave you numb and not able to show emotion. It is important that you do not judge yourself during this phase. We often think that if something happens on a global scale where many people are killed that it is sad but it doesn't affect us. Psychologists have reported many cases where the shock and often post-traumatic stress disorder set in, even if we don't have a connection to the event. Compassionate and empathetic people will feel these effects

Anger: Guilt is usually listed as second, but as mentioned, there is no "right way" to respond to grieving. Have you ever been angry with God or your higher power when someone passes? You don't understand it, and you question, "Why this person? Why now?" In the future, you may feel guilty about these emotions, but please don't get stuck in guilt. Guilt is a very normal response, especially when someone is young or in a tragic accident. When in this early part of grief, people are not looking for the silver lining or how your life will one day be content again. People are simply trying to feel and deal. We need to be careful, as the anger generated from guilt can result in your life being altered forever.

Acceptance: This is when you accept that the person isn't coming back. The emptiness is lifted, and we learn to have a new relationship with the person who has crossed to know how to communicate (talking out loud), and we are no longer angry they are not here with us. It is not to say we are glad they are gone, only that we accept it, and it doesn't control our lives. Many of you reading this book may still not be at this point in your grief process, but hopefully through this book and others like it, you will learn to find a small piece of acceptance.

Guilt: Many of you may be wondering why I place this after acceptance. For many people, the guilt level of grief is very difficult to get through. We feel guilty because we feel somehow we could have stopped it (usually with suicide). If someone was left with the impossible responsibility to decide when life support should be removed, people wonder, "Did I do the right thing? Did I just kill someone who could have lived? I should have taken them to the hospital. That could have saved them." We play games in our heads of how we could have or should have helped or corrected a past action—and we do this all day, every day. Guilt is something that will hinder us from moving to the acceptance level. If you are not celebrating a holiday or have decided not to make cookies that you made with your mom because it causes you a great deal of pain to remember and you think it would hurt your mom to celebrate without her, I'd like to ask you to reframe your thinking. Your mother is happy, and it is important for you to continue the tradition with her and learn how to enjoy doing that activity with her spirit. When you realize you can still have some part of her with you, it is a powerful healing tool to get through this level.

Why do we often get stuck? When someone crosses over, it's hard to imagine them never being in physical form again. No more phone calls, hugs, dinners, advice, and quality time. It's sad, and you are allowed to feel that loss. Your feelings are valid. As you go through the levels of grief, however, and realize that your people are not spiritually gone, it does make life not only more tolerable but also more enjoyable. You are not alone! This is not to say your loved ones are always with you. No one is with you all the time except your guides. As you get to know the signs your loved ones are delivering and celebrate the traditions you once shared with them, you realize that you will continue to have a relationship with them. While it is not the same as being able to pick up the phone, it helps greatly to realize that you are not abandoned.

Most importantly, you *will* be okay! As terrible as you feel when you first lose someone, I promise you that if you allow the grief process to unfold, you *will* be okay. The question that you have to ask yourself is, do you *want* to be okay? The obvious answer to this question is yes, but do we really think about that question and what it really means? You have to want to be okay, to actively participate in being okay and continue to be open to the signs that your loved ones who have crossed are showing you.

Chapter 6

REINCARNATION

$\mathcal{J}$f you would have asked me that twenty years ago, I might have given you a different answer than the one I am about to give you. My father crossed in February of 2001. In late November of 2001, I was in Cincinnati on business. I had gotten back to my room at the hotel and was prepping for bed. I wasn't drunk or sleepwalking. The phone rang. This irritated me since I never gave anyone my hotel number. I assumed it was the kitchen calling me at 11:45 p.m., so I wasn't thrilled. I answered the phone with an abrupt hello, only to hear what sounded like plates and typewriters. I said hello again but even a tad more abruptly, and I heard my dad say, "Lori, honey." Of course I hesitated before saying, "Dad," he then proceeded to tell me that he had tried to contact me before, and he was coming back to make things right. Then the phone did the *doo doo doo doo* sound. I sat there for what seemed to be hours but was about thirty seconds before hanging up the phone. I realized what my dad meant by coming back.

We are told there is heaven and hell and that is it. What I didn't account for was this coming back thing. I have taken the time to ask your people what exactly that means and why that happens. My guide was actually very precise and helpful. If you don't get it right, you come back and do it again. In my dad's case, he was an alcoholic along with a few other issues that made his life choices with people not the best. Reincarnation is something that in each life we learn the lessons that we are supposed to learn. Some of us have lived countless lives and even remember our village or place of our last life. Past life regression is amazing to find out what some of these lives were and who we were. In some cases, the person regressing you can even help you understand how you crossed.

It can also help explain things in some cases where the doctor can't explain why you have a pain in the upper part of your back. You go for test after test, only to hear that there is no explanation why your back hurts. You go to a regression session and learn that in the last life, you were shot in the back and killed. Some of that past life energy is with you and remains in the tragedy spot of your body. There are ways of clearing that up. You can see a Reiki master to help heal that wound that is left from that life.

Reincarnation is not always for the person who

didn't live the best. It can also be that the lesson you were supposed to learn in that life was not learned. This can also be a reason you don't hear from your people. If your person has been reincarnated, then you won't hear from him or her again until both of you have crossed.

Chapter 7

GUIDES

J mentioned earlier veil three is where our guides reside. I am fortunate to be able to see my guide and interact with him daily. The biggest question I get is, "How can I find my guide?" This is not a simple question, so let me elaborate and help you get prepared for the task.

Often people are excited to find their guides. While I understand that excitement, you can't will your guides to appear. Let me be clear what I mean by that. Your guides are always there, but to be connected, you have to be in a place of vibration to receive them. Now I threw a new word at you this chapter, and that is *vibration*. We all vibrate at various levels throughout the day. Our vibrations are affected by food, stress, health, and just daily living. If you are excited or anxious to see your guide or guides, your vibration is much higher. When you are able to experience your guides, you can't vibrate on a high level. Ideally you want to be in a meditative vibration so you can receive the information you want from your guides. Often people will use qualified healers to balance their chakras or get a Reiki session or two to help fine tune them.

Seeing your guide is not as simple as just wanting to see them. You have to be willing to hear and actually listen to them. You may not like what they have to say all the time. If you are in a bad relationship and your guide is telling you to leave that situation and you feel as though you can't, you're not going to listen. I always say be careful what you ask for from your guide. Most of us want to hear what we want to hear, but often our guides are there to keep us from continuing to make the same mistakes. Intuition is often a big sign from your guides. How many times have you really wanted something and your gut steers you clear of it, but you fight your instinct and go with your heart? Fast forward a bit later and you say, "Man, I should have listened to my instinct." Well when you experience your guides, you better be ready to actually listen to them! Once you have accepted all of the possibilities of what the guides may tell you, then you can start your meditations to ground and balance you. Consider your vibration a tree. Trees have a firm root system to stay grounded and branches that allow for the free flow of that vibration. Are you a tree or a cloud? Weird question, right? If you are a cloud, you're not going to see your guide ever. A cloud has no root system and floats and changes all the time. If you are constantly in your head thinking and worrying and trying to look for an easy answer then forget the idea of ever seeing your guides. If you are a tree and start your meditations and gratitude in the morning and evening, then you start to find that balance. Once you achieve that balance, you begin to see the world in a whole new light and experience the world at a balanced vibration.

This is not something that happens overnight, so patience and balance are the keys to success. You can go to reputable healers to help find that balance, but I say the journey is yours to find your guide. You will be able to experience them when the universe says you are ready, not when you want it to happen.

Guided meditation works best for newcomers to meditation. Find an amazing guide to help with meditation that centers and balances you. If you have thoughts of things you need to do or bills that need to be paid in the beginning, it's fine. Never try to focus and forget since that is the total opposite of meditation. Most people will tell you to let your thoughts float out to the horizon like a cloud. I find that acupuncture helps in the areas of release as well and primes you for meditation. Remember, finding your guide is a journey, not a race. If you have some pressing issue in your life and you want help from your guide, it will never happen that way. Slow and steady in the journey will teach you much more than you bargained for on your journey to find your guide.

Chapter 8

DEMONOLOGY

At least once a week I get the question, "Are there evil spirits?" The answer is yes. Since the beginning of time, there has always been a yin and a yang, a good and evil. To balance the universe, you have to have both to create the vibrations that exist in life. We come across people in our daily lives that we have a bad feeling about or just something about them rubs you the wrong way. This is different than a demonic spirit. When I am called in to do a demonic cleansing, it is far more serious than having a bad feeling in your home. In some cases, the most vulnerable person in the house is affected by the entity. This can present itself in several ways, but several of the most common are strong urine smells, bite marks, bruises, scratches, uncontrollable anger, etc. This is often a sign of a portal that allows these beings in your realm. This is not something I recommend handling yourself since it can be very strong and you risk possession. When I come in, I do far more these days than just sage and holy water. The first line of defense for some is having a priest bless the home. I highly recommend saging your home monthly if you can to rid of any negative energies left behind from people who may visit your home. I have learned a great deal over the last couple of years about how strong these demonic energies can be. It's not like the movies, and I would hardly classify them as fun. It isn't something that you can tag along for or watch out of entertainment. I used to do just the basics of cleansing (sage, holy water, blessings, candles, and stones). Now I have a whole new level of understanding of what these entities are capable of doing. Each individual case is accessed first to get the severity of the case before anything is done at all. If it is an energy that has been put on you (curse) or an entity that is there, this greatly affects the next steps.

I always encourage staying positive and not fighting in the home during a home or spirit possession. The anger is fuel to the fire and can make it ten times worse for your actual health. If your house is new and something is going on, please don't tell me that you don't understand it because the property is new. Your land is not new, and even if you have land records, I promise that you don't have a clue what has happened on that land over the last couple thousands of years. I am not an antique collector, but many of my friends are. I always advise them to use extreme caution collecting antiques and make sure to please cleanse them. Mirrors are a prime example of something that creates havoc in a person's home. Think of a mirror as an energetic sponge. If the mirror was in a place where someone was murdered, for example, the mirror will often absorb that energy. If you bring the mirror to your home and start fighting with your spouse, weird illnesses can present themselves and nightmares can begin. I am not discouraging you from collecting, but please cleanse them when you get them home. You can cleanse by using sea salt water, and if the item is small enough, I would say to sit it out on the full moon for a proper cleansing.

Chapter 9

PSYCHIC KIDS

There have been many books published as well as television shows that have covered this topic. I myself have two children who have the intuitive ability. My daughter is nine years old, and like me, she has been experiencing activity since she was about five. She has a different kind of ability. I hope one day she will help others on a global scale. She has recently started experiencing mass tragedy before it happens. This is not a dream state but one that comes out of the blue a few days before the event occurs. She does not see the event from a bystander's prospective. She sees the event as a victim of whatever tragedy she is experiencing.

There was a mass shooting in Orlando, Florida, at a nightclub a few months back. This is the first time she experienced what I would call a global alert. She came to me hysterical and said that she saw in man in red coming toward her, and then it went dark. She stated that it sounded like fireworks, but she was scared and could hear people screaming around her. I assured her that she was fine and that together we would work on figuring out what it all meant. This was honestly a first experience for her, so I didn't have much to go on as to why or what had just happened. A few days later prior to hearing the news of the terrible tragedy in Florida, she stated that she was feeling better and not upset any longer. Later that day I was alerted to what had happened in Orlando. It was as though her anxiety had disappeared after the person whose view she was seeing this from crossed over.

In a cynical way, I chalked it up to her being sensitive and kind of a fluke experience. A few months later, once again she came to me in a hysterical way just like before. This time I went into protection mode, and we meditated on where this was. She said it was near the Eiffel Tower. Two days later in Nice there was the tragedy of a man who ran a large amount of people over with a box truck. She once again felt better after the event occurred. I have reached out to some of my psychic friends who have studied this specific ability in kids. She, in fact, has a prophetic gift that many of us are born with but later shut down as we grow older. I cannot stress enough to you to be open to your children if they come to you and tell you they saw someone or know something is going to happen. I am a firm believer that if you shut off your ability that you live with anxiety the rest of your life. I have seen this happen to countless people in their late sixties and seventies. They have come to me and said they never spoke of the things they saw as children because their parents never believed them.

There are a few things to look for that I can speak directly about with my experience and my daughter's. If you have a child who talks to you about seeing your father who passed, and you know he or she has never met him in this life, I encourage you to allow your child the freedom of telling you about their relationship. So many people think their parents didn't get to see their kids when, in fact, they see them often. They may talk to you about night terrors. This is a tricky area of actual nightmares and possible negative entities. If the night terrors continue, I would encourage you to seek someone in your area who specializes in children with psychic abilities. If your child speaks of an imaginary friend, perhaps it his or her guide or a friend who passed with him or her. Please be patient and allow your child to be open with you. I cannot stress this enough. Your patience and understanding may very well help your child learn what he or she has is not bad or evil. When you are a parent/guardian who has the ability to help a child process an amazing gift he or she has, educate yourself so you can do so in a healthy way for everyone involved.

Kids are overmedicated these days beyond belief. I won't get on a soapbox about this, and I think there are valid reasons they should have medication. If they are seeing people you can't, taking them to a doctor who prescribes an anti-anxiety or anti-depressant medication to make it stop is where my big concern is. Medication is only a Band-Aid for stopping something that they are born with, therefore creating additional anxiety and eventual health issues.

Chapter 10

GRATITUDE AND MANIFESTATIONS

If you get nothing else from reading this book, please take away the importance of gratitude and manifestations. This section can change your entire life going forward. How many times have you said, "This sucks" or "I hate my life" or "I can't" or "Why me? I just want to be happy." or "Why can't I catch a break?" or just about anything else negative you can throw in here? I know for me the list is endless, just like everyone reading this. Positive thinking is hard to maintain all the time. Some days it's hard to think positive at all. Life happens, and things often don't go as planned, so thinking it's roses and sunshine is more than just a simple task.

Let me briefly explain why the negative thinking and speaking aren't going to change anything for you. Now most of you are thinking, *I know that*, but it still happens. The universe is the most powerful and amazing place, and it has an abundance just waiting for you. Now some of you equate abundance with money or finances, but that is not the abundance I am speaking about.

The abundance the universe has is one of ask and you shall receive. Please don't be over the top and think that if you ask to hit the Powerball, you are going to automatically win millions. I am not saying you are not capable of winning, but I always counsel people to make their goals attainable. I'm talking about things that are core to your being and that you believe win with your head and your heart.

It's important to remember that the universe works in both positive and negative outcomes. If you are looking for a relationship and ask for an amazing mate who is caring, loving, and loyal and then think at the same time that it will never ever happen because you have never had a good mate in the past and they don't exist, then you will never find that relationship because you don't actually believe it exists. You are simply reinforcing the negative. You need to focus on the positive!

And please be specific as well. You can't say, "I just want to be happy." What is happy? Happy is a broad statement, and quite frankly, the word doesn't mean much. Be present and very aware of what specifically makes you happy. Don't just say that you want peace because again, what does peace look like to you?

This process is often made easier and more specific by creating a vision board. On that vision board, make sure to get a variety of colors to represent the areas in your life that you are trying to work on. Love, for example, to me is red or pink. Money is usually green, for obvious reasons. On the board, put a picture of you in the middle—a recent photo of yourself that you feel shows confidence and happiness. Then get your colored pencils out and go to town on compartmentalizing your life. Your life is like an onion and needs the layers peeled back so you know what you really want to put out to the universe in the first place. The more detailed you are, the better it is, not to mention this also gives you a better insight into who you really are. This process often helps us better understand ourselves as it demands specific details. Let's say you want a new job that pays more money and is closer to home. While that is relatively straightforward, you need to add what else you want from the job. Do you seek growth? A 401K? Vacation time? Nice coworkers? Your own office? Flex time? Let's remember that you have to be fully detailed with everything you want. When I do this exercise with some of my clients, they think they know exactly what they want until we delve deeper. This is an amazing exercise that everyone should experience to really get more familiar and specific about that they want from their time here on earth.

It is also a great exercise for overcoming grief and maintaining that new relationship with your loved ones who have passed. Why do you want them to visit? What answers do you feel you need from them? As mentioned earlier, they are not coming with some powerful words of wisdom or giving you permission to move forward. They are fine, more than fine; they are amazing! Of course, you miss them being in physical form, but if you get stuck on what life was like with them here, then you are staying stuck and missing out greatly on the relationship you could be having with them now.

Life is in the details you create. Please do not be a rubber band that wants positive but thinks negative. Rubber bands break because they are stretched too thin because they are pulled too far in both directions. Manifestations are amazing when you realize that *you* hold the key to your peace and happiness. Wow, pretty powerful stuff. It's not easy, but powerful to know that no matter what cards you were dealt in your formative years, you have the opportunity to control your own destiny.

Simply put, manifestations are actually the law of attraction.

Let me expand on the concept of the law of attraction. I'm sure this is not a new concept for most of you. If anyone has ever read the book *The Secret*, then you have a clear idea as to what I am talking about. The simple concept is what you put out comes back to you. While this seems easy enough, so many people have no idea how to truly use the law of attraction. The key is always being aware that everything you do contributes to what you manifest.

The universe gives what you ask for. So before you say things about a cheating husband or never finding a relationship that works, what are you actually putting out there? In the case of the cheating husband or spouse, remember that you can't control others or their actions. In theory we all want to have our cake and eat it too. I am pretty content in my little world with my family and have no desire to have more than one mate, but for many they would like to have more than one. This comes in to play when you say, "If John was only more like Steve," so it would be an ideal mix if you could take them and mash them together. Since that isn't possible and you want a mate who is kind, honest, caring, and respectful, then that is what you have to put out. I always say to start with a vision board. You can create this to be any way that you would like it to be, but I say to get a large poster board and a new pack of colored pencils. In the middle of the poster board, I recommend getting a recent picture of you that you feel as though you were confident and strong. Please do not get a picture from thirty years ago when you were nineteen years old and thin just because you want to be thin again.

Once you have that picture, put it in the center of the board. Each section of your life that you want to work on will be in a different color. You can use whatever color you want for each section. I will reiterate the colors I use on my boards. Money is green, love is pink or red, family is light blue, career is dark green, health is yellow, spirituality is orange. You can make any category you would like and you can make it any color as long as each section is a different color. The different colors will allow you to compartmentalize your life and not live so stressed in your mind. So in the case of a relationship, what exactly is it that you are looking for?

When dealing with the universe, you *must* be specific! Don't use words like happy on your board please. Happy is a general term that can be taken in many different ways. What makes me happy might not make you happy and vice versa. When I talk to most of my clients, I find the word *happy* used often, and many times people aren't even sure what makes them happy in the first place. When you have the categories for your boards then you will begin populating each section with pictures and desires for that particular section. In the case of love, what is it that you really want out of a relationship? I say to write ten things in two columns in each section if you can. I know ten seems like a lot, but the more you put out to the universe that is detailed, the more you will receive what you are seeking. The first column is for things that you are nonnegotiable on. This would be something like respectful, honest, caring, etc. I say list at least five things in the first column that you are not going to budge on and would be a deal breaker if they were not those things.

The second column is for things you desire but are willing to negotiate on, like height or weight. This really helps in law of attraction because you are still putting out your idea of a perfect mate for you. In each section you will do this exercise, which may take days to do. You will find that when you separate things in your head that it isn't so easy to describe what you really want. One of the hardest things is to compartmentalize what you truly desire. Career may have an aspect of financial, but it is still different in many ways. Career will give you the ability to put down what kind of work atmosphere you would like, along with vacation time, flexibility, and location. Money has to be realistic please.

Once your board is completed, which again may take days or weeks to complete, then keep the board where you can see it each day. I recommend doing them each quarter or at least twice a year. When things you desire happen or your desires change, then so should your boards. Okay, so now you have the board and you have compartmentalized everything, so now what? Let's be clear that the universe does not have a time reference and the biggest and hardest part of the whole exercise with the board is to actually let go and believe it will happen. If you write it down and then think about how each relationship has been a bad one and you were cheated on, then you're likely to get another just the same. Trust and letting go is one of the hardest things any of us do in life. It means we have to be vulnerable and exposed, which can be very difficult if we have been hurt or let down in the past. The law of attraction is one of the most powerful free tools in the world. If you write all this down on the board and then assume it isn't going to happen, it won't. That is pretty easy and basic I know, but if you stay open and let the universe work the way it is supposed to, it will.

This can also help us move forward in the moving on phase as well. When you are stuck, what are you stuck in? This does not only reference people who have crossed but your day-to-day life that feels boring or too routine. When you complain, remember that is put out to the universe as well. I fall victim like everyone else but have to remind myself that if I stay in that mind frame then I will never get out of it.

Let's use the example of a friend who has hurt us after we have been open and vulnerable with them for so long. The Buddhist religion has an amazing way of looking at these situations. Remember that anger is a secondary emotion to fear or hurt. You own your own anger and allow it to control your life. I am not saying we all have to skip along the rainbow with glitter and unicorns, but if you allow that anger to move you, then you are the only one who suffers the pain. There is no one in this world you should allow to control what you put out to the universe except you! I know that can sound selfish if you have children, but the reality is each of us are individuals who have to focus on our own vision boards of life. You can't control your kids when they grow up, and you can't and shouldn't control another person.

When working with the universe, be direct, harmless, open, and realistic. If you stay present and give to the universe what you truly desire, the universe will give back to you openly and honestly.

FAQs

Do I believe in God?

Most certainly! I am spiritual but do not follow organized religion. My personal belief is that each religion tailors certain rules within the church. I talk to God daily and have great gratitude and appreciation for all he does for me and has blessed me with. God can be called a higher power or higher spirit. I have been told by high people within the Christian religion they do believe I have a God-given gift.

How will I know if someone is around me?

I have found there are about ten most frequently used methods. There are more, but these are the ones that are used the most. Keep in mind there are others that are not listed here simply because they are less frequent, and in all honesty, there is something new I learn from them all the time.

Butterflies

They choose butterflies to let you know they are free. They have explained it to me in a way that I find so comforting. They say that when we are here in veil one, we are caterpillars. When we become ill, we are in a cocoon, and when we cross to veil two, we are free like the butterfly. I always recommend that if you have been told that your loved one brings butterflies then grab a butterfly bush and plant it in the backyard. Not every butterfly is a sign, but it doesn't hurt to have the reminder that often you are not alone.

Electricity

This is what I would consider to be the most *common* one. Now if there is a storm outside and the electricity goes off, don't read more into that. It's just a storm causing the electricity to go out. This kind of visit is very subtle. It is small surges or flickers when you are *talking out loud* and need advice or guidance. This can affect anything electrical—cell phones, radios, and even temperature changes in the house. If you can keep a journal of when these things happen, it's amazing to see that they are often there when you need them the most.

Time

This goes hand in hand with electricity, only they mess with clocks. I always think this one is cool. There is no time where they are, and when people use this one, they will say it's to let their people know they will be there till the end of time, etc. Pay attention to clocks. They will stop the time if only for a brief moment or mess with the microwave clock and make it blink. The same applies here to the storm or electrical surges. If there is a storm, then it is just a storm. Sometimes we want a visit so bad we will wish everything as a visit. If your loved one was a clockmaker or collected watches, then often this is the mode they choose

Dimes/Silver Coins

We have all heard the saying, "Pennies from heaven." Maybe so, but as for your people who have crossed, they don't seem to send pennies. They usually send dimes, nickels, or quarters. Dimes seem to be chosen most frequently. I have asked why. I would love to give you an amazing answer, but I know ten is a whole number, and from what I understand, it is used the most because it's a whole number to them. There is no huge revelation other than you find them when you are seeking answers from your loved ones. Men seem to choose this the most. This is not to say that your female loved ones never come this way, but most of the time this is from males who have crossed. If you can, put the dimes in a separate jar as you find them. It's always nice to see that they are around more than you think and you can measure it by your visit jar.

Move Things

This happens to so many people who think they have gone batty. Subtle visits are sometimes hard for you to see or recognize. People have reported things moved the next day, cabinets are opened, keys appear under pillows, and blankets are moved. It is not to say that sometimes you just forget where you put something, but often when you see a trend of things being moved, you are being visited by someone who is trying to get your attention.

Cardinals

Cardinals are angel birds. Cardinals actually have a short life span but are considered angel birds in veil two. While other birds can also be a sign of a visit, cardinals represent the tranquility where they are. This also often means they want you to be more peaceful for yourself, so slow down. Women tend to be the culprit behind this. As mentioned with butterflies, get a bird feeder that attracts the birds. This again does not mean every red cardinal you see is your grandmother, but having the energy of the birds around can be quite soothing.

Hummingbirds

We all love cute little hummingbirds. This seems to be similar to the butterfly, only no cocoon. If Grandma chooses this way of letting you know she is around, it is to let you know she is free. Hummingbirds, however, while appearing slow are actually very fast-moving little guys. Your people say when they visit this way, they are letting you know they are calm and tranquil and you are going too fast and need to slow down. I had an amazing woman who had crossed over tell her daughter once that she needed to stop moving her wings so fast. I later found out that the woman had two jobs and was a single mother. Her mother's message was very powerful and has since helped her slow down and focus on her.

Dreams

This is one I get asked about the most. We have all had dreams of our loved ones and woke up excited that Grandma just visited us. Maybe she did, but let me explain how that works. If you have a dream and Grandma meets you in a park where there are trees and grasses, then yep, consider that a visit! If she meets you at the mall and there are no trees or grasses, then sorry, that is just wishful dreaming. I do know that they are drawn to the trees and other elements after they cross over. I do not have any answer as to why that is, but I do know that if they are in the elements, you have gotten a visit from Grandma.

Scent

I know before anyone comes through for me I always get their scent or a scent that is attached to them (food, cologne, etc.). I have had people actually smell them too while in a reading. It is always fun to see their faces when they smell the pot roast I smell from grandma. Everyone had a scent or two that people associate them with. Some can be laundry, pasta sauce, cookies, breads, and any other scent you remember them for. The scent will be brief.

Shadows

This one is a little less frequent than the others, but it does happen. The shadows will be either up really high near the ceiling or very low toward the ground but always fast. We often blame the dog, cat, or kids for these shadows, but it's a lot different than the dog running through the house. It's much faster. Do not freak out. Just acknowledge that you know someone is there. Often what your people want you to know is they are there. This will present itself to a lot of people who could once see spirits as children and chose to try to shut it off. You can never fully shut it off. Shadows are not always bad just because they present in black usually.

CPSIA information can be obtained
at www.ICGtesting.com
Printed in the USA
BVOW08s2259230317
479344BV00001B/1/P